P9-DEL-374

CHANGING OUR WORLD

H. NORMAN SCHWARZKOPF

E. J. Valentine

A BANTAM SKYLARK BOOK®
NEW YORK • TORONTO • LONDON • SYDNEY • AUCKLAND

**To the fighting spirit of the men and women of Operation Desert Storm.
Special thanks to Doris Thomas at Fort Rich
and Dean Wohlgemuth at Fort Stewart.**

RL 3, 007-011

H. NORMAN SCHWARZKOPF

A Bantam Skylark Book/September 1991

Skylark Books is a registered trademark of Bantam Books, a division of Bantam Doubleday Dell Publishing Group, Inc. Registered in U.S. Patent and Trademark Office and elsewhere.

Produced by Angel Entertainment, Inc.
Cover design by Joseph DePinho

ISBN 0-553-15967-4

Published simultaneously in the United States and Canada

Bantam Books are published by Bantam Books, a division of Bantam Doubleday Dell Publishing Group, Inc. Its trademark, consisting of the words "Bantam Books" and the portrayal of a rooster, is Registered in U.S. Patent and Trademark Office and in other countries. Marca Registrada. Bantam Books, 666 Fifth Avenue, New York, New York 10103.

PRINTED IN THE UNITED STATES OF AMERICA
OPM 0 9 8 7 6 5 4 3 2 1

Contents

Background 1

Chapter 1
A Very Young General 5

Chapter 2
War in Vietnam 21

Chapter 3
Code Name Urgent Fury 39

Chapter 4
Operation Desert Shield 56

Chapter 5
Operation Desert Storm 76

Quick Facts 97

Chronology 98

Index 101

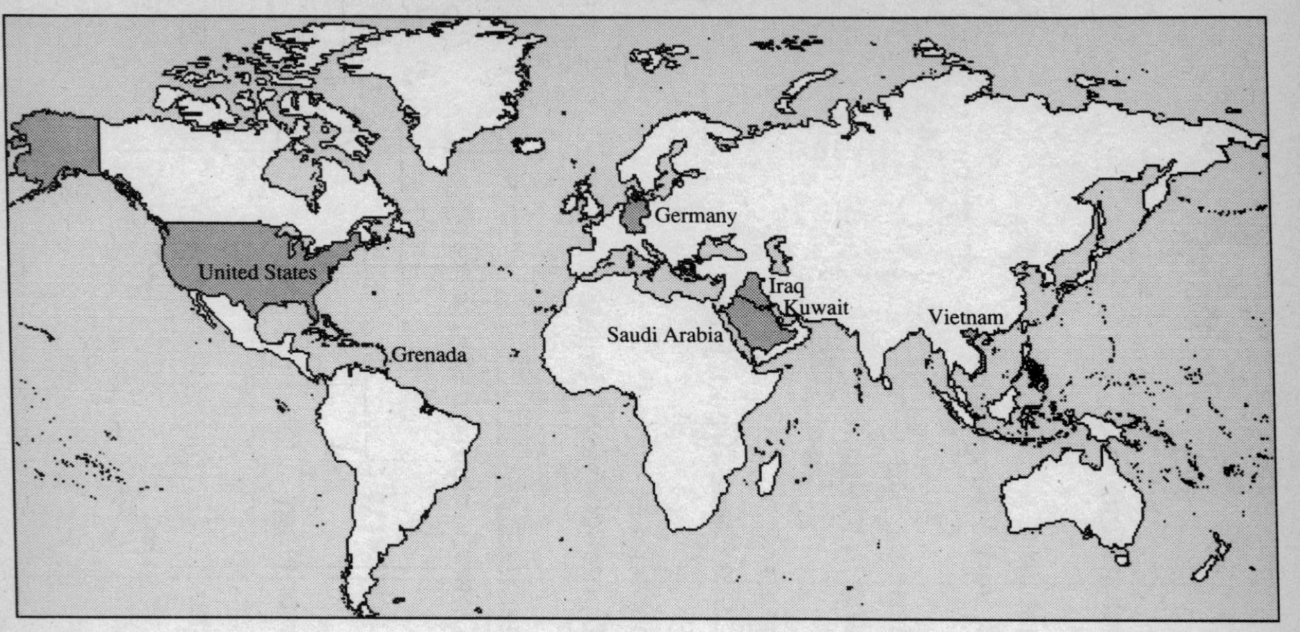
Germany
United States
Iraq
Kuwait
Vietnam
Saudi Arabia
Grenada

United States of America

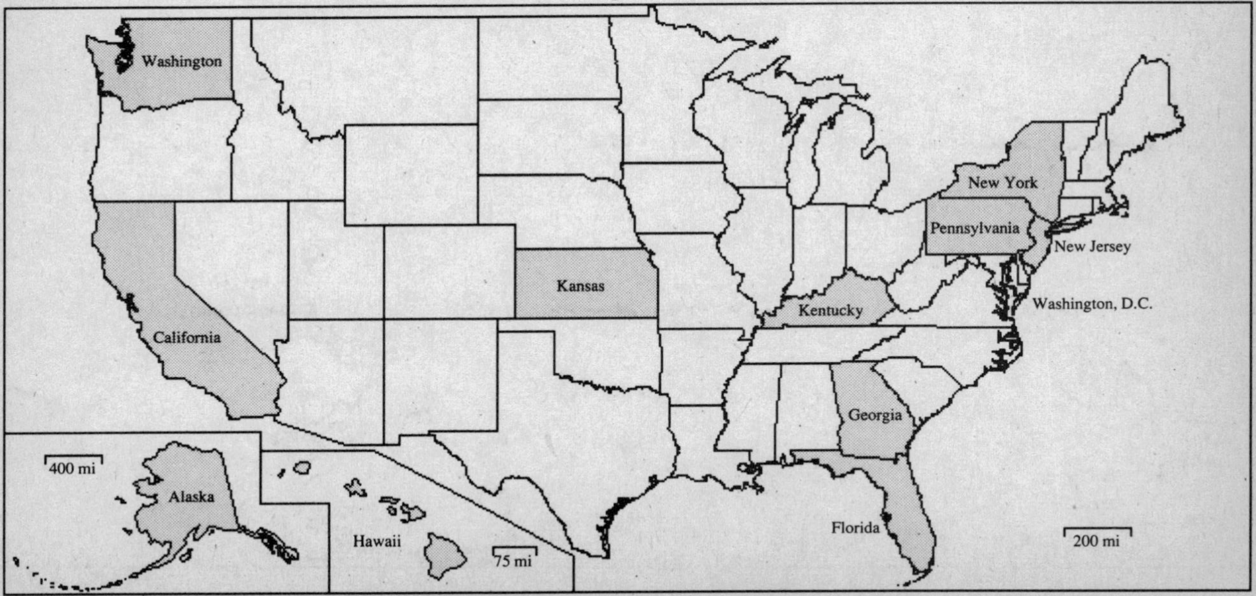

Background

Many great American generals have led the armies of the United States in battle. Without them, America could not have been victorious.

In 1775, at the start of the American Revolution, George Washington was named commander in chief of the Continental Army. Although Washington was not a great tactician, he was nevertheless the force behind his troops. After suffering near devastating defeats in 1777, General Washington and his six thousand soldiers camped for the winter at Valley Forge near Trenton, New Jersey. Many men had no shoes, no trousers, and no blankets. Weeks passed without proper food, so men were forced to boil their shoes in order to eat the leather.

In spite of these conditions at Valley Forge, Washington instilled true discipline in his men by teaching them how to fight. They practiced rigorously, especially hand-to-hand combat, and learned how to use bayonets. The events of that winter have become a symbol of wartime suffering, courage, and perseverance. In 1781 Washington led the army that emerged from Valley Forge to victory at Yorktown, ending the war.

Like Washington, General Ulysses S. Grant was fiercely loyal to his cause during the Civil War. He knew how to rally his troops, and led the armies of the North to victory over the South. Even though the North had more money and men, it was not an easy victory. The South was led by a brilliant tactician, General Robert E. Lee who became legendary for his mastery of the art of warfare.

At the outset of the war, Grant was not a master at tactical planning and strategy as Lee was. But he understood his enemy and the fact that Southerners believed that their very way of life was on the line in the war. Grant knew they would fight to the end. Calm in a crisis, Grant did not lose his judgment in the face of his troops' defeat. By destroying Southern economic resources and by cutting off the lines of communication and all supplies to the South, Grant was able to destroy the South's very power to make war.

Victory for the North was achieved in 1865.

General Grant also did something no other general before had attempted. He created one strategic plan that every one of his armies was to be a part of. Each army had a specific purpose in Grant's grand plan to surround the entire South, east of the Mississippi River. This became one of the building blocks of the American Army system.

During World War II the supreme Allied commander was General Dwight D. Eisenhower. This quietly brilliant man was responsible for millions of men and women in the land, sea, and air forces of all of the Allied countries, including the United States, Great Britain, France, and the U.S.S.R. His strength lay in his ability to integrate those forces.

Eisenhower also had the ability to get the best out of the people who worked for him. He encouraged the generals under his command to take control in the field and he gave them free reign. For these reasons, Eisenhower has gone down in American military history as one of the greatest generals of the twentieth century.

When General H. Norman Schwarzkopf attended West Point Military Academy, his favorite course was about great generals. He especially enjoyed learning about generals from American history. Little did he know then that almost forty years later, he would lead the American Army and its allies to a decisive victory in the Persian Gulf War. Along with the campaigns of Washington, Grant, Lee, and Eisenhower, the Persian Gulf campaign led by General H. Norman Schwarzkopf is destined to be studied by many future generations of West Point cadets.

In the tradition of great American military leaders, General Schwarzkopf believed fiercely in his cause and in his soldiers. He was victorious in the quickest, most successful, and most decisive of all American wars. He has been called a "soldier's soldier" and a born commander. This is the story of his life.

1

A Very Young General

At two-thirty in the morning of January 17, 1991, General H. Norman Schwarzkopf assembled the staff of Operation Desert Storm in the War Room in Riyadh, Saudi Arabia. He asked a chaplain to say a prayer of protection for the troops. Then he played one of his favorite songs, "God Bless the U.S.A," by Lee Greenwood. After that he announced simply, "Now, let's get to work."

Ten minutes later Apache attack helicopters of the 101st Aviation Brigade crossed the border into Iraq and fired the first shots of the Persian Gulf War. They were preceded by the ultra-secret MH-53 Pave Low helicopters whose job was to locate enemy radar and destroy it. The night was cold, clear, and very dark. It was three hours until dawn in Baghdad. Operation Desert Storm had begun.

More than one thousand allied aircraft participated in the attack. They came from seven countries: the United States, the United Kingdom, Saudi Arabia, Kuwait, France, Italy, and Canada. They spoke four languages over their radios and intercoms, but they were united in their purpose—to liberate the country of Kuwait.

Miles to the south in those early hours of the air campaign, General Schwarzkopf delivered a message to the troops. As he spoke, pilots listened on their headsets, soldiers on their ham and short-wave radios, and some of the troops read his words in print as they came over fax and teletype machines at their desert posts.

"I have seen in your eyes a fire of determination to get this job done quickly so we may all return to the shores of our great nation," General Schwarzkopf began. "My confidence in you is total. Our cause is just! Now you must be the thunder and lightning of Desert Storm. May God be with you, your loved ones at home, and our country."

The most massive air attack in history had begun. And General H. Norman Schwarzkopf was the field commander, in charge of all operations on the battlefield. It was his job to make sure that Operation Desert Storm went smoothly and successfully, and with the loss of as few lives as possible. It was a general's ultimate challenge.

H. Norman Schwarzkopf was born on August 22, 1934 in Trenton, New Jersey. He grew up in a large cobblestone house on Main Street in Lawrenceville, just outside of Trenton. Norm had two older sisters, Ruth Ann and Sally. He spent more time with Sally because they were closer in age and also because Sally was more of a tomboy. The two of them thought Ruth Ann was prissy because she played the piano.

The only son of an Army colonel, Norm was groomed for the military from an early age. When Norm was four, his father told him that he would follow in his footsteps and go to West Point. Norm was named after his father, Herbert Norman Schwarzkopf. But the "H" in Norm's name doesn't stand for anything because his father hated the name Herbert so much that he refused to give it to his only son.

Colonel Schwarzkopf was young Norm's first hero. Born in 1895 in Newark, New Jersey, Norm's father was the only child of German immigrants. He

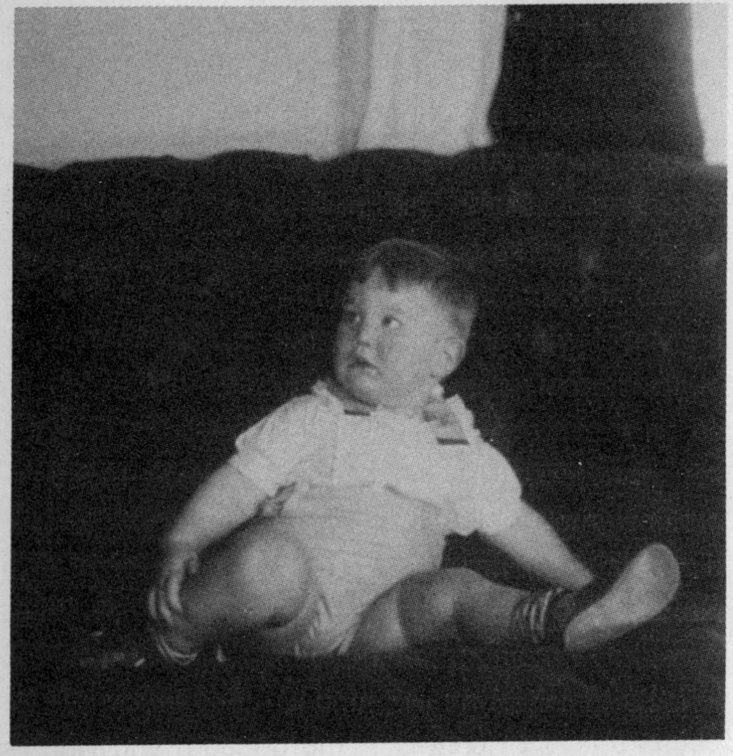

Norm as a young boy, about 1936. (Visions)

graduated from West Point in 1917, where he was called "Schwarzie" and was known for his huge appetite and his skills as a football player and a boxer. His classmates kidded him that he was shaped like a beer keg.

Norm's father fought in World War I until he was injured in a mustard gas attack. During the Allied occupation of Germany after the war, he oversaw the reconstruction of some German towns.

Back home in New Jersey, Colonel Schwarzkopf went on to become the first superintendent of the New Jersey State Police in 1921. He was determined to whip the force into shape and soon developed a test to give police applicants. Colonel Schwarzkopf also designed the triangular badge, still worn by New Jersey State Troopers today. Its three points stand for the three words in the motto he paraphrased from that of West Point: "Honor, Duty, Fidelity." His biography is still included in the state trooper textbook.

The same year that Norm was born, Colonel Schwarzkopf arrested the man he claimed was responsible for the highly publicized kidnapping and murder of Charles Lindbergh's baby. It was one of the most notorious crimes of the decade, and Norm's father led the investigation. The case and Colonel Schwarzkopf received a lot of media attention. Norm's father also became known for hosting a radio series about police adventures called "Gangbusters."

During World War II, when Norm was eight years old, his father was appointed by President Franklin Delano Roosevelt to go to Iran. Every week Colonel Schwarzkopf sent long letters home describing the

Lindbergh Kidnapping

In 1927 the American aviator Charles Lindbergh became the first person to fly across the Atlantic Ocean alone. He won a large amount of money and became an international hero. In 1929 he married Anne Morrow and the young couple spent the next few years flying all over the world, mapping new routes for airlines. On March 1, 1932 the Lindberghs' twenty-month-old son was kidnapped from their home in New Jersey. Ten weeks later his body was found. After two years of investigation, led by Colonel Schwarzkopf, the New Jersey State Police arrested a man named Bruno Richard Hauptmann for the murder. He was convicted and executed in 1936.

art, music, people, and culture of Iran. He usually closed with personal notes for each family member. To his only son, he wrote, "Norm, take care of my girls."

At the age of ten, Norm was sent to Bordentown Military Institute, near Trenton, New Jersey. When photographs were taken for the yearbook, the ten-year-old cadet insisted on posing for two pictures, one smiling and one grim-faced. He explained: "One day when I become a general, I want people to know that I'm serious."

When Norm was twelve, he joined his father in

The Schwarzkopf family in New Jersey in 1941. Norm is standing next to his sister Sally, on the right. Ruth Ann is on Colonel Schwarzkopf's other side. (Visions)

Iran. The two of them hunted wild animals and toured the country. Norm even accompanied his father on some diplomatic missions. Once he was actually served sheep's eyes. He debated eating them until his father gave him a look that said that not only was he to eat them, he was to eat them with a smile.

Norm at about age eight. (Visions)

Six months later his mother and sisters joined them. Norm and his sisters attended a Presbyterian missionary school. The family moved to a house so large and luxurious that it was like a palace. They had a chauffeur, chef, butler, laundress, and garden boy who came when they were summoned. Less than a week after they had arrived, however, Colonel Schwarzkopf called his three children together and warned them not to ring any bells or give the servants any orders. He reminded them that they were still middle-class Americans who took out their own garbage and looked after their own needs.

In 1947, after Norm's father was promoted to brigadier general, the family moved to Geneva, Switzerland. Norm and his sisters attended an international school with children from many countries. Norm learned French, played soccer and tennis, and lived in the boys' dorm at the school. He did not excel academically, although he has an IQ of 170.

When General Schwarzkopf was transferred to Germany, he enrolled Norm in a school in Heidelberg. Norm joined the student council, played a lot of sports, and learned German. Like most teenagers he loved to exasperate his parents. One weekend he was grounded for having missed his midnight curfew.

He sat in the family music room and played "Home Sweet Home" on an accordian until he drove his mother crazy.

When he was fifteen, the family returned to the United States. Norm went to Valley Forge Military Academy in Wayne, Pennsylvania. He was nick-named Hugo by his classmates because of the rumor that the "H" in his name stood for that. He lived in Wheeler Hall and awakened every morning to the blare of the bugle. Despite the strict rules of military school, Norm and the other cadets could not resist starting food fights in the cafeteria once in a while.

In his senior year Norm was elected class valedictorian. He was a champion debater and also starting lineman on the Valley Forge football team. The football coach said he never had to yell at Norm, but he admitted that Norm played better when his temper flared. Norm took orders well, but sometimes questioned why he was being asked to do something.

Norm started at West Point in 1952. He was given the same nickname his father had had thirty years earlier: "Schwarzie." Norm spent his first eight weeks living through a time known as "Beast Bar-racks." Along with his new classmates he underwent initiation into West Point, known to all the cadets as

Norm at a shotput event at Valley Forge. (Courtesy of Valley Forge Military Academy)

"hazing." They were forced to march endlessly and repeat ridiculous phrases and do other silly things that the upperclassmen demanded. Norm was made to repeat the opening of "Gangbusters," his father's old radio show. Norm would stomp his feet and imitate the wail of sirens and the rat-a-tat of machine guns.

Hazing is a tough time for cadets at West Point. They are given a lot of abuse by the upperclassmen to see who is tough enough to take it. The cadets who don't make it through hazing are then asked to leave the academy. Norm managed to make it through.

West Point is famous for providing fine military training and for its strict honor code. The motto of the school is, "Duty, Honor, Country." There are no locks on the cadets' doors because it is expected that everyone can be trusted. The year before Norm went to West Point, there was an honor code scandal. Many cadets were expelled for cheating. The event had a strong impact on all the new cadets in Norm's class, and honor was strongly instilled in them.

Norm participated in lots of extracurricular activities, including wrestling, football, soccer, and tennis. He also belonged to the German club and the weight lifting club. He was commander of his cadet company, and he led the choir in his senior year.

The United States Military Academy

In 1802 the United States created the Corps of Engineers, located at West Point, N.Y. The Corps' job was to set up a military academy to train engineers who would build fortifications for the Army. By 1812 there were eighty-nine graduates. Over the years, West Point continued to grow, adding new types of training and study. In 1976 the academy admitted its first women cadets. To maintain discipline, West Point has a long-standing tradition known as the "honor code." This states that cadets will not lie, cheat, or steal or put up with those who do. The code is carried out by the cadets themselves. Among the great military leaders who have graduated from West Point are: Robert E. Lee, Ulysses S. Grant, Stonewall Jackson, Philip Sheridan, John J. Pershing, Douglas MacArthur, Dwight D. Eisenhower, George S. Patton, and H. Norman Schwarzkopf.

Norm excelled in the mechanical engineering courses, which many cadets dread. These complicated science courses involve the study of physics, specifically Newton's laws of motion. Because Norm did so well in engineering, he was expected to choose the artillery as his military branch since a good knowledge of mechanics is necessary. Artillery is a class of weapons that fire from long distances at targets that canot be seen. Artillery soldiers stand

Norm's graduation picture from West Point. (Courtesy of West Point Military Academy)

behind the main battle lines and pinpoint targets a good distance away in support of the soldiers on the

Military Branches

The following units are put together to form larger ones, such as regiments and divisions:

Infantry units fight enemy soldiers at close range. They enter battle on foot, by helicopter, parachute, or some type of armored vehicle.

Artillery units fire on enemy troops and artillery, using cannons of various sizes.

Armored units consist of tanks and other vehicles with protective armor plate. They support attacks with cannons, missiles, and machine guns, and carry troops.

Army Aviation units move troops and commanding officers around the battlefield and spot targets for artillery. Its planes and helicopters also move soldiers rapidly to safe areas for medical attention.

Missile units provide fire support similar to artillery.

Communications and Observation units send and receive messages, and use radar to detect enemy planes and troops.

Transportation units use trucks, helicopters, amphibious vehicles, boats, and air-cushion craft to move troops and cargo from one place to another.

Logistics units store, package, and supply ammunition, food, spare parts, clothing, and other necessities.

field. Instead of artillery, Norm picked the infantry, a division that requires no specific knowledge of mechanics. Infantry soldiers fight on the ground and engage in direct combat with the enemy.

Norm loved the idea of becoming a "mud soldier." He tried to recruit more of his classmates for the infantry, not an easy task since it was considered the least glamorous and most dangerous and physically demanding branch. But Norm knew that it was also the most important branch, since infantry are the troops who do the actual fighting.

Norm graduated from West Point in 1956 in the top ten percent of his class, forty-second out of a class of 485. His entry in the senior yearbook states that his personality won him many friends. It concludes with this line: "His spirit is his greatest asset and will assure him success."

Later this statement would be proven true. Only two members of the West Point class of 1956 would go on to become four-star generals and Norm would be one of them.

2

War in Vietnam

After Norm's graduation from West Point, he was sent to the United States Army Infantry School at Fort Benning, Georgia. This six-month course is a requirement for all Army infantry soldiers. During the first half, soldiers learn military discipline, map and aerial photograph reading, and personnel management, the basics that all Army officers in every branch must be taught. Then they learn more about the branch they have chosen. In Norm's case, it was infantry.

In March 1957 Second Lieutenant Schwarzkopf started his first assignment. He was sent to Fort Campbell, Kentucky, as part of the Second Airborne Battle Group, 187th Infantry, of the 101st Airborne Division. Airborne soldiers are trained the same way

Norm as a second lieutenant. (Visions)

as infantry soldiers, except that they jump out of aircraft and parachute into a battle. Norm's mission at Fort Campbell was to train men, keep morale high, and ensure that the troops were battle-ready. Considered an elite unit because its troops had to be ready to fight any enemy at any time, it was a tough and demanding introduction to the Army for Norm.

As the lowest ranking officer on the base, Norm was in charge of keeping stock of the inventory in the officers' clubs and the commissary; inspecting the mess halls; and serving guard duty. He also had to serve as prosecutor at court martial trials. A court martial takes place when a soldier is accused of breaking Army rules. A trial is then held to determine whether the soldier should be punished, and if so, what his punishment should be. As prosecutor Norm represented the Army and their cases against the accused officers.

Norm served at Fort Campbell for two years. His experiences there gave him skills that would aid him throughout his military career. He learned how to manage supplies, how to command soldiers, and how to help those soldiers deal with their problems. He also learned military justice firsthand.

Norm's next assignment was in Europe as part of the Second Battle Group, Sixth Infantry. He served there for one year, starting in July 1959. He moved up from Platoon Leader to Liaison Officer to Reconnaissance Platoon Leader and later Liaison Officer, Headquarters. A liaison officer is someone who helps one type of unit work with another.

In July 1960 Lieutenant Schwarzkopf was appointed as aide-de-camp to the commanding general at the Berlin command in Germany. This meant he would be working very closely with the general. Norm would get an inside look at high-level operations from a general's perspective. And because many more military maneuvers were conducted in Europe than in the United States, Norm would get firsthand experience of how maneuvers should be run.

In September 1961 Captain Schwarzkopf was chosen to attend the Infantry Officers Advance Course at Fort Benning, Georgia. This was a sure indication that he would be promoted to major. After that Norm was selected to go to the University of Southern California to study mechanical engineering.

Norm received his Masters degree in June 1964, and was then assigned to teach mechanical engineering at West Point. He was supposed to teach for three years. As it turned out, he taught for only one because of the outbreak of the Vietnam War in 1965.

Norm believed in his country and in the Vietnam

War. He felt that the United States was coming to the aid of a weak democracy, the Republic of South Vietnam, which was under attack by its stronger Communist neighbor, North Vietnam. Norm heard antiwar protestors claim that the United States had no reason to be in Vietnam because they were unjustly interfering with another country's civil war. But Norm felt the protestors were more worried about being drafted themselves than about what was right and what was wrong.

Norm's assignment in Vietnam was to be a field adviser to Vietnamese airborne troops. This was a difficult and dangerous post. Norm's job was to get his troops to fight as well as possible. But most of his men did not speak English, which caused some communication problems. In addition, Norm and his troops had to travel through enemy territory, which was filled with land mines. Snipers hid behind trees and bushes, lying in wait to attack. Norm slept on the ground with his men and ate rice with chopsticks. He even wore a South Vietnamese uniform so as not to stand out, even though he stood six-foot-three compared to the average Vietnamese soldier's five-foot-three.

In spite of the hardships, Norm considered this

The Vietnam War

In 1954 Vietnam was divided into two parts, North and South. The Communist government of the North wanted to bring the South under its control. In 1954 the North attacked the South, and the United States sent military advisers to South Vietnam. Gradually more and more American troops were sent, until the number reached 530,000 in 1969. But U.S. military assistance could not make up for the weaknesses of the South Vietnamese government. In addition, many Americans protested against the war, and President Nixon finally began to withdraw U.S troops in 1969. Peace talks between the two sides failed to stop the fighting, and in 1975 the North captured the capitol of the South and the war ended. The toll was nearly 55,000 American dead, plus 150,000 wounded. The South Vietnamese lost tens of thousands of people as well, and the North admitted to over half a million men killed.

first tour of duty one of the most rewarding experiences of his life. He was exposured to Vietnamese culture and he also learned a lot about what it was like to live in a different culture and how to adapt to it.

During this tour Norm won two silver stars and two purple hearts for bravery. He won one of his silver stars while on a mission in enemy territory to locate some missing troops. When he found them, he

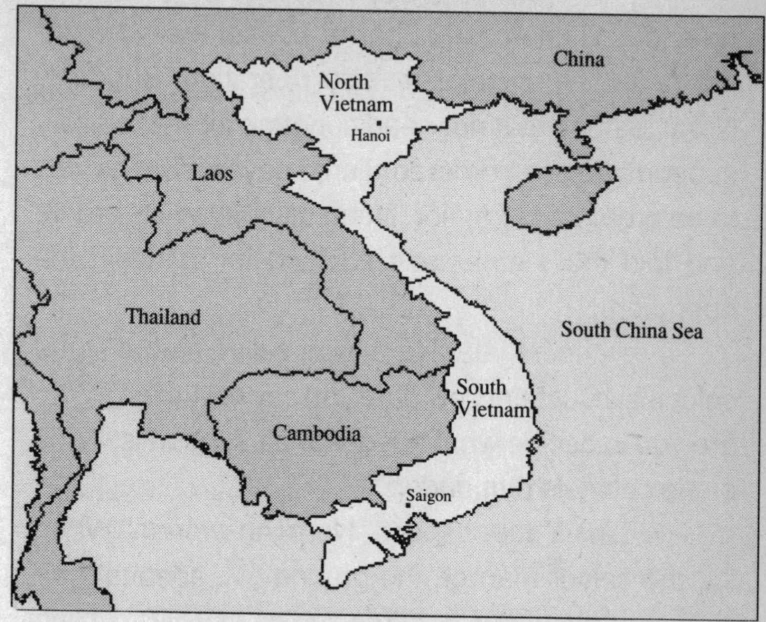

North and South Vietnam during the war.

treated their injuries and then led them to safety. Another time during a North Vietnamese assault, he rushed through enemy fire in order to figure out the enemy plan of attack so that he could best direct his own forces. During this conflict he was wounded four times, but he refused to be evacuated or to take cover until his mission was accomplished.

Just as he had sometimes questioned authority as a young cadet at Valley Forge, Norm challenged his orders when he felt the lives of his men were at stake. During a campaign in Ia Drang Valley in 1965, he and a Vietnamese airborne adviser were preparing to launch a major military operation. Suddenly Norm learned that not nearly enough air and artillery support had been ordered. Three days before he was to be promoted to major, Norm disobeyed his orders and told the Vietnamese adviser not to begin the operation.

A few hours later Norm was called before some colonels. "Captain, how dare you say not [to] go? Who are you to decide what adequate air support is?" one of the colonels demanded.

"Sir, in all due respect," Norm answered. "When I'm the senior man on the ground . . . adequate air support is about one hundred sorties of B-52s circling my head all in direct support of me. I may be willing to accept something less, but that's just barely adequate when it's my butt on the line."

During this first tour, Norm became more and more concerned about the attitude of his superiors. They didn't seem to care about the needs of the men in the field. An example of this occurred at the Duc Co special forces camp in the Vietnamese highlands. Norm and his troops had just spent ten days in a major battle, surrounded by thousands of enemy soldiers. Wounded Vietnamese were lying all over the ground.

Silver Star

This military decoration is awarded in all the armed services. It is given to men and women for heroism in combat and is the fourth-highest award in the armed forces.

Purple Heart

This decoration is awarded to all members of the American armed forces who are wounded in combat. The heart-shaped medal bears a portrait of George Washington and hangs from a purple ribbon.

Norm was on the radio frantically trying to get some helicopters to land and evacuate his injured troops.

Now that the battle was finished, there were many helicopters flying around, but they were all busy transporting officials. Norm grew so frustrated that he started cursing over the airwaves. A relief unit finally arrived along with the commander of U.S. advisory forces in Vietnam. Many reporters were with him, and they wanted to interview Norm. The commander asked to speak to Norm first before he met with any of the reporters.

Norm was exhausted and dirty from ten days of battle so he figured the commander wanted to give him a pep talk. Instead the commander simply asked him if the mail had gotten through during the fighting.

Norm helping a wounded paratrooper at Duc Co. (AP/Wide World, 1965)

Norm said the incident crushed his spirits. The commander didn't seem at all aware of what Norm had just been through.

In June 1966, after a year in Vietnam, Norm returned to West Point as an associate professor. A year later he met Brenda Hoslinger at an Army football game.

Originally from Timberville, Virginia, Brenda lived in New York City and was a TWA flight attendant. She and Norm began going to movies and taking walks in Central Park. Two months after their first date, they were engaged. On July 6, 1968 they were married in the West Point Chapel.

After a honeymoon in Jamaica, Norm was assigned to the Army Command and General Staff College at Fort Leavenworth, Kansas. He was also promoted to lieutenant colonel over a lot of other officers.

Norm was sent to Washington, D.C., in June 1969 to serve as executive officer to the chief of staff who oversaw military operations in Vietnam. One of the chief's primary duties was to direct all the soldiers in Vietnam. Norm hated sitting behind a desk, but he picked up useful information about the war as well as details about the movement of troops.

Wedding of Norm and Brenda at West Point Chapel in the summer of 1968. (Visions)

In December of that year, he was finally given a field command in Vietnam again. He said good-bye to Brenda and took command of a famous infantry battalion known as the Americal. During the course of the war, the Americal won eleven medals of honor. Brenda did not see her husband for one long year except for a brief visit in Hong Kong.

Norm was awarded his third silver star during this second tour. The incident took place when one of the companies under his command accidentally walked into a mine field. Some of the soldiers were wounded, including the company commander. When Norm's helicopter landed there, a young private stepped on a land mine. The blast hurled him into the air and he fractured his leg. He lay on the field, screaming in terror and pain. Slightly wounded by the explosion, Norm made his way cautiously across the mine field.

When Norm reached the private, he spread his body over him so that he wouldn't move and injure himself further. Then he ordered four other men to cut a limb from a nearby tree so that he could use it as a splint for the private's broken leg. One of the soldiers stepped toward the tree and triggered another blast. Three of the men were killed instantly, and one was severely wounded. Norm successfully rescued the private and won another silver star. But the horrible experiences he endured on the battlefield would leave an impression on him for the rest of his life.

Norm found this tour of duty grim. The jungle was hot, filled with leeches, and there was little good drinking water. His troops were poorly trained for battle, although they had already engaged in fighting. He was again bothered by the easy living of his superiors and their lack of concern for soldiers in the field.

Norm felt, as many other soldiers did, that the

military pressured officers to make sure there were high enemy body counts. By reporting that a lot of the enemy had been killed, certain high-level officers tried to demonstrate that their forces were doing their jobs. Some defenseless Vietnamese peasants, including women and children, were actually shot in order to increase the enemy body counts. Norm was disgusted by this brutality.

There was also concern that the number of American casualties, especially those by "friendly fire," was being concealed. Friendly fire is the term used to describe what happens when soldiers are accidentally shot at by other soldiers on the same

How to Tell the Rank of a U.S. Army Officer

Rank	Insignia on Uniform
Second Lieutenant	single gold bar
First Lieutenant	single silver bar
Captain	two silver bars
Major	gold oak leaf
Lieutenant Colonel	silver oak leaf
Colonel	silver eagle
Brigadier General	one silver star
Major General	two silver stars
Lieutenant General	three silver stars
General	four silver stars
General of the Army	five silver stars

side. Friendly fire was responsible for the deaths of many soldiers during the Vietnam War. Norm was criticized for one incident in particular.

In February 1970 Michael Mullen, a twenty-five-year-old sergeant from Iowa, who was under Norm's command, was killed when an American artillery shell exploded above the pit where he was hiding. His parents received vague letters signed by Norm, but no one would give them any details about how their son had died. Eventually they discovered that their son's death had not even been listed because it was not battle-related. They wondered if the Pentagon was purposefully making it seem as if the number of American deaths was lower than it actually was.

C.D.B. Bryan, a writer for the *New Yorker* magazine, wrote a book based on this incident called *Friendly Fire*, which was later made into a TV movie. After extensive research, he concluded that Mullen's death had been completely accidental. Although Norm was technically in command, he had not been on the scene, so he could not be blamed. It also came out that Norm had never signed or even written the vague letters sent to the Mullens. They were written by someone above him in Washington. Norm had in fact been denied permission to write a letter to the

Mullens. The *New Yorker* writer portrayed him as a courageous and honorable officer.

Norm returned to the United States in July 1970. He was shocked by the almost hateful treatment of Vietnam veterans. Many people thought that the U.S. was making a terrible mistake by taking sides in the war. War protestors often blamed soldiers for decisions made by the government. As a result, soldiers felt betrayed by their country. Norm didn't know what to think. He had been taught to follow orders, but his experiences in the war filled him with doubt about being in a job that often required killing human beings.

His daughter Cynthia was born that August. Norm's job was in the Office of Personnel Operations at the Pentagon. His mission was to see that infantry officers were educated and trained, and then to make sure that the right officers were picked for training at the right times in their careers.

In 1971 Norm entered Walter Reed Army Medical Center for back surgery. His back had bothered him since high school when he had played football. Parachute jumps and leaping in and out of helicopters in Vietnam had not helped either. His spine had been fractured, and the doctors were not sure whether the operation would be successful.

Norm was lying in a hospital bed in a body cast when the Mullens called him. They had tracked him down and now threatened to take him to court for what had happened to their son. Norm talked to Mrs. Mullen over the phone and asked that she and her husband come to see him so they could discuss it face-to-face. Norm cried as he tried to talk to them about the Vietnam War, but the Mullens were not moved.

Norm's back healed and he stayed in the Army, but the scars of the war lingered. One day that spring, his sister Sally came over for a visit. A war movie happened to be on TV, so Sally, Brenda, and Norm watched it. Norm grew visibly agitated as they watched the soldiers in the movie going through a mine field.

Sally asked him how he was feeling. Norm tried to explain the horror of war and how upsetting it had been to watch young men die for a cause that had become less and less clear. He added that it had also been difficult to return home to the American public's total lack of support.

Sally said that she felt that the peace protestors did have a point. Norm lost his temper, burst into tears, and ordered her to leave the house. He called her later to apologize, but it was clear to him that he had not come to terms with his experiences in Vietnam. Norm was still confused about what the Army had been doing in Vietnam. The Vietnam experience had definitely tarnished the Army's reputation, making it seem as if all soldiers were bloodthirsty killers of innocent people. He thought about quitting the military altogether.

He decided that he knew one thing for sure. If he ever had to compromise his principles to stay in the Army, he would hang up his uniform.

It was a difficult time to be in the Army, but Norm was not a quitter. The time to walk away, he concluded, was not when everything was broken. Instead he'd rather walk away when things were fixed. Someone had to help fix the Army. Norm decided to stay.

3

Code Name Urgent Fury

After two years in Washington in the Office of Personnel Operations, Norm was chosen to attend the Army War College at Carlisle Barracks, Pennsylvania. It was a definite signal that he would soon be promoted to full colonel. Norm found his ten months there relaxing, interesting, and educational. He wore civilian clothes and participated in lively round-table discussions. There were also many guest speakers. Norm knew, as everyone in the Army knows, that Carlisle is the breeding ground for future generals. The course ended in June 1973.

Then he returned to the Pentagon and served as an assistant in the Financial Management Office in Washington, D.C. He reviewed Army budget pro-

Norm and Brenda with their daughters, Cynthia (left) and Jessica (right) in 1974. (Visions)

posals, hoping to get assigned to a field command again.

Finally his wish came true. In the fall of 1974, Norm became the deputy commander of the 172nd infantry brigade at Fort Richardson, Alaska.

Under Norm's direction the troops worked hard. They drilled endlessly, ran difficult field exercises, and engaged in mock battles. He even had them build ice bridges over rivers. Norm wanted them to be the best cold weather unit the Army had ever seen.

In August 1975 he made the four thousand troops under his command participate in Ace Card Chulitna, their toughest challenge yet. Ace Card Chulitna is a war game designed to train soldiers in the art of mountain fighting. Since no one knows which team, or army, is going to win the "war," the same kind of surprise attacks occur that would during real battles. The soldiers marched seventy-five miles in three days. Then they engaged in eleven days of simulated battle exercises.

"Automatic reactions keep people alive in combat," Lieutenant Colonel Schwarzkopf said. "Half the point of this exercise is making the mistakes now under blank fire and not later." Although war games are serious business, Norm showed his sense of

Norm hiking during Ace Card Chulitna in 1975. (Courtesy of Fort Richardson, Alaska)

humor after the men on his team successfully cut off the other team's supply lines. He sent the opposing team's commanding officer a piece of jerky along with his best wishes and an antacid tablet.

Norm loved Alaska. He spent a lot of time outdoors. One weekend he had Brenda drop him off by the Resurrection Pass Trail, which he planned to hike by himself. Thirty-eight miles long, the isolated trail is dotted with streams and populated by moose. It rained all weekend. When Brenda finally picked him up, Norm was sitting by the side of the road with a big smile on his face.

Norm also did a lot of salmon fishing. Besides steak and mint chocolate-chip ice cream, salmon is one of his favorite foods.

In the fall of 1976, Norm was appointed commander, First Brigade, Ninth Infantry Division, at Fort Lewis, Washington. The three thousand soldiers under his command engaged in simulated combat and quickly found out how tough and demanding he was. One officer claims that Norm got the name "Stormin' Norman" during this time because of the way he barked out orders to his troops.

From July 1978 until August 1980, Norm served as deputy director for plans, United States Pacific

Command at Camp H. M. Smith in Hawaii. His son Christian was born in that same year. Norm also became a brigadier general.

In his job he met with representatives from the Pacific nations and worked as the United States liaison with the Pentagon. This meant that he was the point of contact between Washington and the Caribbean. He also developed military, political, and economic policy. Although the job was prestigious, Norm did not have any soldiers to command. As usual, he could not wait to get back in the field again.

After Hawaii Norm was sent to Mainz, West Germany, to serve as assistant division commander, Eighth Infantry Division, United States Army, Europe. There he worked closely with some of the military's brightest soldiers. He also earned his second star. He was now a major general.

The Mainz unit was revolutionary at the time because it had a unique mix of high-technology, excellent training, and talent. It was there that the Army introduced equipment that could imitate lifelike combat. This equipment allowed Norm's soldiers to gauge the accuracy of their shooting. Norm's experiences at Mainz would prove invaluable to him in later years.

After two years as assistant division commander, Norm was sent back to the Pentagon in August 1982 to serve as director of Army personnel. He was back at the same place he had worked ten years earlier, but this time he was in charge. Norm developed procedures and legislation affecting the physical and mental standards of all Army officers.

After only ten months Norm was assigned to command the Twenty-fourth Mechanized Infantry Division at Fort Stewart, Georgia. This is one of the biggest divisions of mechanized infantry in the Army and is among the first to go into combat. Norm would have 14,400 soldiers under his command.

Norm was excited about his new assignment. It was the first time he would have complete command of a military post. He and his family drove to Georgia with their entire menagerie of pets. There was Bear, Norm's black labrador retriever; a cat; two parakeets; and a gerbil.

The day Norman took command of the Twenty-fourth, he made a speech that people still remember. He talked about how good the Army was. Then he said that "The U.S. would carve a 'V' [for victory] in the face of any enemy that dared to challenge the Twenty-fourth division."

In October, after he had been at Fort Stewart for only four months, he received a phone call from the Army Forces Command in Atlanta. Norm was informed that he had been chosen for an important military operation, but was given no other details except that he was to report to Atlanta at once. When he left the house later that night, he had no idea what he was getting himself into.

Norm arrived in Atlanta at 10:15 P.M. on Sunday, October 23, and found out that he had been nominated to serve as deputy commander for a highly secret operation that was code-named Urgent Fury. He had been picked for the job by General Richard Cavazos, his former division commander at Fort Lewis. Cavazos was convinced that Norm was a born leader who worked his troops hard and got results. The Pentagon was reluctant at first to take Norm away from his post at Fort Stewart, but Cavazos convinced them that he was their man.

The goal of Operation Urgent Fury was to invade the island of Grenada in the Caribbean. The United States had been asked by the Organization of Eastern Caribbean States (OECS) to participate in the invasion. Its purpose was to restore democracy to the island and eliminate Cuban interference there.

A communist revolutionary force had recently overthrown the government and then executed Maurice Bishop, the head of the government. The Grenadians were afraid of what would come next.

On top of that there were over one thousand American students living in Grenada, attending medical school. Another equally important aim of Operation Urgent Fury was to rescue these students. President Reagan and his advisers felt it was likely that the students would be taken hostage.

On Monday morning Norm met Vice Admiral Joseph Metcalf III, commander of Urgent Fury. The two of them were flown by helicopter to the U.S.S. *Guam*, which was anchored off the shores of Grenada. They worked together in a small compartment near the bridge of the ship. Metcalf said that Norm was so big he took up half of the space all by himself. The operation was planned in a matter of hours, not nearly enough time to coordinate things properly.

The invasion was scheduled to begin at 5:00 A.M. the next day. The plan was simple: Army Rangers were to air-drop onto the airfield at 5:00 A.M. and secure the area. The most elite Army unit, Rangers are trained to fight in the heart of enemy territory.

Grenada

This tiny island nation in the West Indies achieved its independence from Great Britain in 1974. With a population of about 100,000, the people are mostly of African or mixed African-European descent. English is the common language. In 1979 a group of Communist rebels overthrew the government and put in their own prime minister, who established close ties with the Communist government of Cuba. Then in 1983 Grenada's revolutionary leaders killed the prime minister because they thought he was not converting the island to communism fast enough. Other Caribbean countries became worried that Grenada would be used by Cuba and the Soviet Union as a base for revolution and terrorism, so they asked the United States for help. On October 25, 1983 American forces invaded the country, assisted by troops from six Caribbean nations. After a short conflict with Grenadian communists and Cuban soldiers, order was reestablished. A new government was elected in 1984.

Then after the Rangers had done their job, they would be relieved by troops from the Eighty-second Airborne. Early the following morning, Marine units were to launch an assault by sea and take one of the airports.

But things did not work out as planned. The Rangers were not able to land on the airfield because

Cuban construction equipment was in their way. They had to parachute drop instead. Then, as the planes flew in, they encountered heavy fire from antiaircraft guns. Some pilots were able to drop despite the antiaircraft fire, but others had to abort the mission entirely. After fighting the Cubans on the airfield, the Rangers finally managed to capture it.

The Rangers then proceeded to the main campus where the medical students were supposed to be. When they got there, they found only 138 students instead of the 600 they expected. It turned out that, contrary to the U.S. intelligence reports, the main campus was located elsewhere. They reported their findings by radio to the *Guam.*

When Norm heard what had happened, he was furious. He could not believe that there was such a gap in intelligence, or information. Their primary objective had been to rescue the students, and then it turned out that nobody even knew where they were. Metcalf explained the confusion by saying that Grenada had never been a U.S. intelligence priority. Not a lot of attention had been paid in the past to what was happening there.

It seemed as if things were not destined to run smoothly. That same afternoon, two special oper-

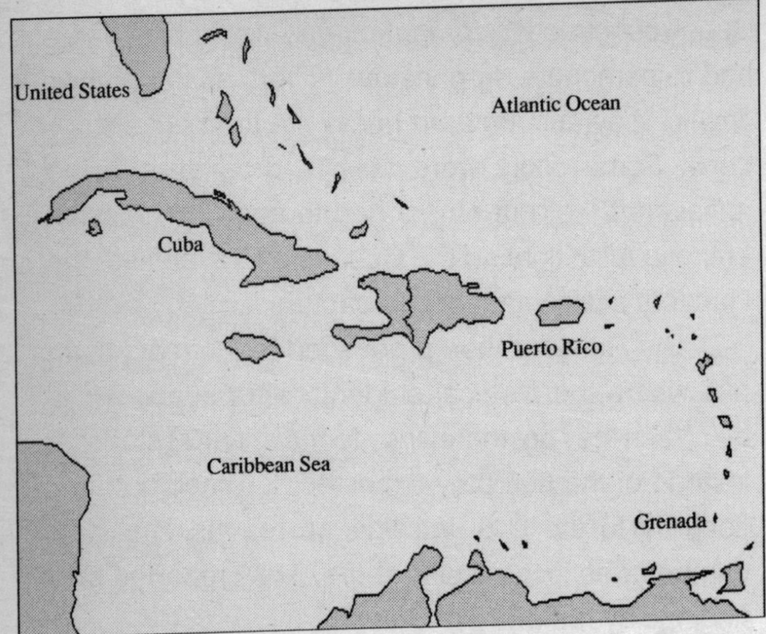

Grenada and the Caribbean Region

ations helicopters were supposed to rescue a British government official who had been placed under house arrest by the revolutionaries. But the troops walked into a trap and needed to be rescued too. At the same time, Norm and Metcalf realized that they had too much of their force on the northern half of the island and not enough on the southern.

Norm then came up with an idea that would turn the tide of the invasion. He suggested that the Marines make an assault from the sea to rescue the trapped forces and then secure the surrounding area. Marine advisers didn't like his plan, however, because the beach where the Marines would have to land had not been surveyed. It was definitely a risky maneuver, but Metcalf decided to listen to Norm and go with it.

Metcalf first ordered an air attack. In that action, two helicopters were shot down and a psychiatric hospital was hit by mistake, causing the deaths of about thirty patients. But the Ranger units were making progress against the Cubans and the rebels in the south. By afternoon 150 Cubans had been captured.

After the air attack, Norm and Metcalf met to discuss plans for day two. Metcalf decided to make Norm his deputy commander for the rest of the operation, although some felt that this position should be held by someone actually on the island. Metcalf, completely impressed with Norm, stood firm.

By the next morning it was clear that Norm's idea to move the Marines had been a good one. Five M-60 tanks and thirteen amphibious landing vehicles went ashore. They advanced according to plan, and soon secured the general's house where the forces had been trapped.

Next Norm turned his attention to the Army

forces. They were supposed to make a land assault, but had yet to reach their destination because they were bogged down with the fighting in the south. Norm started to get angry. He was worried that they might not make it to the campus before dark to rescue the students. In the heat of his frustration, Norm came up with a solution. He would use Marine helicopters to transport Army Rangers to storm the campus, while Navy planes covered the operation from the air.

The joint operation lasted for only twenty-six minutes. It went off almost perfectly, and 223 Americans were rescued. After only nine days the Grenada invasion was declared a success, despite the hasty planning and numerous mistakes.

The Grenadians sang "God Bless America" as the American troops prepared to return home. Their happiness affected Norm deeply. When he spotted red graffiti on a wall in Grenada he was sure, after his experience in Vietnam, that it would say something negative like "Down with the U.S." Instead it read, "God Bless America."

Upon his return to the States, Norm was nervous about the American response to the invasion. At the airport he was surprised to be greeted by family, friends, and a military band. He said the experience was one of the greatest thrills of his life.

Back at Fort Stewart Norm threw himself into training the troops of the Twenty-fourth Infantry. He continued the Emergency Deployment Readiness Exercises (EDRE), designed to keep the troops battle-ready. Soldiers were required to report to their unit directors with no prior notice, and then prepare to move out within twenty-four to seventy-two hours. They loaded tanks and equipment onto ships, and then off-loaded at specified destinations, as if participating in an actual war. When the operation was finished, they proceeded to Fort Bragg for war games.

Under Norm's direction the troops were instructed to paint all equipment desert camouflage, as opposed to the normal forest green. The part of the world they were being trained for was the Middle East, an area predominantly filled with deserts.

Norm devoted himself to keeping his soldiers physically and mentally fit. Described by many as a "soldier's soldier," he was primarily interested in improving the lives of the men and women under his command. While at Fort Stewart he initiated the "Fit to Fight" diet, a low cholesterol, low fat, low salt diet. The idea took hold and spread until it became used

Army-wide. He also initiated construction for a new enlisted men's club near the barracks.

Congenial and outgoing, Norm was loved by the soldiers. He was also respected for never using his status to his advantage. While at Fort Stewart he bought some furniture and a boat, but he introduced himself to the merchants as Norm, not as General Schwarzkopf. To this day at Fort Stewart, he is remembered for never putting on airs.

In 1985, after two years at Fort Stewart, he was sent back to the Pentagon as assistant deputy chief of staff for operations and plans. One of the most prestigious offices in the Army, it was also a signal to Norm that bigger things were to come.

In June 1986 Norm was promoted to lieutenant general and given the command of I Corps at Fort Lewis, Washington. This time he was in charge of an entire infantry corps. He worked his troops hard, but as he had at Fort Stewart, he also looked for ways to improve their lives. He made recreational activities like skeet shooting affordable for his troops.

Many soldiers remember him arriving at the skeet range with his dog, Bear, and his son, Christian. Bear soon developed a reputation for not being well-behaved. Norm tried to keep him in line, but Bear refused to listen to his orders. Norm confessed that he had already sent him to obedience school once, and it looked as if he might have to send him again. He was extremely proud, though, of one trick Bear could do. Norm would open a can of soda, pour it toward the ground, and Bear would swallow every drop.

In August 1987 Norm was sent back to the Pentagon to serve as deputy chief of staff for operations and plans. Although he didn't like being back at a desk, he knew that the job was a very high honor. Norm was the number two man in the entire Army, and responsible for all operations. It was a time-consuming job and Norm worked fifteen-hour days regularly. He went to lots of meetings and waded through lots of paperwork. He did not get to see his family nearly enough.

In November 1988, during this command, Norm was awarded his fourth star. He was also appointed commander in chief of the U.S. Central Command. This job would soon thrust him into the public eye and become his biggest challenge yet.

4

Operation Desert Shield

When Norm took over United States Central Command (CentCom) at MacDill Air Force Base in Tampa, Florida, in November 1988, there was a big ceremony. Over three hundred spectators attended, including thirty generals. All four services—Army, Navy, Air Force, and Marines—marched in formation. There was a nineteen-gun salute in honor of visiting Defense Secretary Carlucci. The secretary praised CentCom and Norm's predecessor, General George Crist, for helping to keep peace in the Persian Gulf.

The United States has ten unified commands made up of all four services. Each command has a commander in chief (called cinc, pronounced "sink") and is responsible for monitoring the military

Joint Chiefs of Staff

This group of military men advises the U.S. President, the secretary of defense, and the National Security Council. It consists of the chiefs of staff of the Army and Air Force, the chief of Naval operations, the commandant of the Marine Corps, and is headed by a chairman and a vice-chairman. The chairman outranks all other officers in the four services and is the top military adviser to the president. The joint chiefs prepare military plans and direct the various military commands that work for the secretary of defense.

situations in a specific part of the world. CentCom is responsible for an area the military calls Southwest Asia, or the Middle East.

The staff at each command works on creating plans in case of war in any of their areas of responsibility. A commander in chief is in charge of the combat forces if there is a war. CentCom is responsible for military operations in eighteen countries, including Kuwait, Iraq, Iran, and Saudi Arabia. But CentCom is based in Florida, seven thousand miles away from its area of responsibility.

Norm made a point of touring all the CentCom offices within his first month and meeting most of the staff. He put a stop to the excessively long working hours and encouraged his staff to exercise and spend more time with their families. He turned the annual CentCom family day into a major event with a picnic and a carnival, instead of just having an open house so that kids could see where their parents worked. As the father of two teenaged daughters, as well as a thirteen-year-old son, Norm knew what kids liked.

Working at CentCom also gave Norm the opportunity to spend more time with his family after the grueling hours he had worked at the Pentagon. He hiked and played tennis with his children and shot skeet with Christian and Bear. Florida was the fifteenth place the Schwarzkopfs had made their home. They acquired some new pets while they were there, including a scorpion and a python.

Shortly after taking command, Norm and his staff looked at the existing plans for war and then began to design all new plans. They decided that the most likely troublemaker in the Middle East was Iraq. This country had recently negotiated a cease-fire with Iran after a nine-year war. And now the Iraqi army of nearly one million men and very sophisticated weaponry was free to fight elsewhere. There had already been a number of border disputes between Iraq and Kuwait over the possession of certain oil refineries. Iraq posed a threat to the oil fields in Kuwait and Saudi

Oil Makes the World Go Round

In the 1850s it was learned that oil from under the ground was excellent for lighting and for lubricating machinery. The first well to pump oil was built in Pennsylvania in 1859. Soon the rush was on. People were prospecting for oil throughout the United States. With the invention of the internal combustion engine, the need for "black gold" grew. Automobiles, ships, and the new airplanes could not function without it. In the l920s oil was discovered in the Middle East, particularly in Saudi Arabia, Kuwait, and Bahrain. As the black, sticky liquid became more and more necessary for modern life (plastic is made from oil), its value increased. Warfare became increasingly dependent on oil because ships, planes, and tanks use fuel in enormous quantities. This means that countries with large underground supplies can become very wealthy and powerful. But if one country or group of countries controls too much oil, others may feel threatened.

Arabia. The danger was clear.

Although the United States had supported General Saddam Hussein al-Takriti, the president of Iraq, in his war against Iran, the U.S. was suspicious of what he might do now that the war was over. Iraq had to pay back a huge war debt from the war with Iran, and Saddam needed to sell oil to raise the money to do so. Kuwait, one of the most oil-rich countries in the Persian Gulf, was producing too much oil, lowering the price. This angered Saddam.

Norm and his staff started planning for what the U.S. would do if the Iraqi forces tried to take over the Kuwaiti and Saudi oil fields. At the end of July 1990, Norm put a number of his troops through an exercise to test readiness for desert action. Called "Internal Look 90," the exercise was intended to run through what the United States would do if Iraq invaded Kuwait. Based on a computer war game, the exercise would shortly become the Pentagon's plan for Operation Desert Shield.

Five days later, just after midnight on August 2, 1990, Saddam launched a massive attack on Kuwait. By late afternoon he had taken Kuwait City. At this time Kuwait had about twenty percent of the world's oil reserves, but it was a tiny, almost defenseless country. Saddam's 95,000 troops easily overwhelmed Kuwait's 20,000-man army.

Norm had just finished a workout when the "hot line" phone in his bedroom rang. It was Colin Powell, the chairman of the Joint Chiefs of Staff. "They just crossed the border," Powell informed him. Norm immediately changed out of his sweaty clothes and went to work. As the United Nations Security Council met to discuss what was happening in the Middle East, Norm and his staff reviewed their plans. The nightmare Norm had predicted since taking command of CentCom had happened.

By August 5, only three days later, the Iraqi army had advanced to within ten miles of the Saudi border. Saudi Arabia had the largest oil reserves in the entire Middle East, at least two and a half times as much oil as Kuwait.

Norm flew to Washington on August 3 to meet with President Bush, Chairman Powell, Defense Secretary Cheney, and the National Security Council. When it was Norm's turn to speak, he laid out his plan based on "Internal Look 90." He said that to defend Saudi Arabia, the U.S. would have to immediately send at least 140,000 men and women to the Middle East. Some of the people at the meeting were shocked by the amount of force Norm wanted to use.

President Bush was thinking along the same lines, however. He believed that it was vital that the U.S. not just sit back and allow a brutal dictator to upset the delicate balance of power in the Middle East. He agreed that a massive buildup was the way to go. But he was worried about one thing—the

The President of Iraq

Saddam Hussein was born in 1937 to a peasant family, but his parents died when he was still very young. As a young man he joined the Baath political party, which supported the idea of unity among all Arabs. In 1959 he was part of a group that tried to assassinate Iraq's dictator. The plot failed and Saddam had to escape to Egypt. When the Baaths seized power in 1968, Saddam returned and became a powerful leader of the party. In 1979 he took control of the country and immediately began to kill and imprison people who might oppose him. With a steady flow of money from the sale of oil, Saddam built up the Iraqi army and started a long, bloody war with neighboring Iran. He has used poison gas on both his enemies and his own people and is reported to have personally killed many political enemies. Under Saddam many Iraqi people live in terror.

Saudis had not officially asked for help.

The next day Norm went to Camp David for another meeting. He laid out his plan more specifically, using flip charts and graphs. He spoke with the unique blend of warmth, common sense, and military language that would become his trademark. President Bush was impressed. He decided that along with Defense Secretary Cheney, Norm was the man to go to Saudi Arabia and meet with King Fahd, the ruler of that country, to discuss the Persian Gulf situation.

On August 5 the president formally announced that he would not accept anything less than a complete Iraqi withdrawal from Kuwait. The United States had taken a definite stand.

On August 6 Cheney and Norm met with King Fahd at his palace. They explained the situation as the U.S. viewed it. Norm added that he was worried that Saddam could fire Scud missiles with chemical warheads at Riyadh, the capital of Saudi Arabia. King Fahd, after listening to Norm and Cheney, decided to invite the U.S. forces into his country to defend his kingdom.

The following day President Bush announced that Operation Desert Shield had begun. Its goal was to deter and repel Iraqi aggression, and to restore the government of Kuwait.

Bush ordered several thousand American troops to the Persian Gulf. Britain and France also sent ships. The forces allied against Iraq would be known as "the coalition." Although the allied coalition included many nations, not all of them sent forces to actually fight. The bulk of the fighting forces came from the United States, Saudi Arabia, the Arab Gulf States, Britain, France, Egypt, Syria, and Pakistan. In

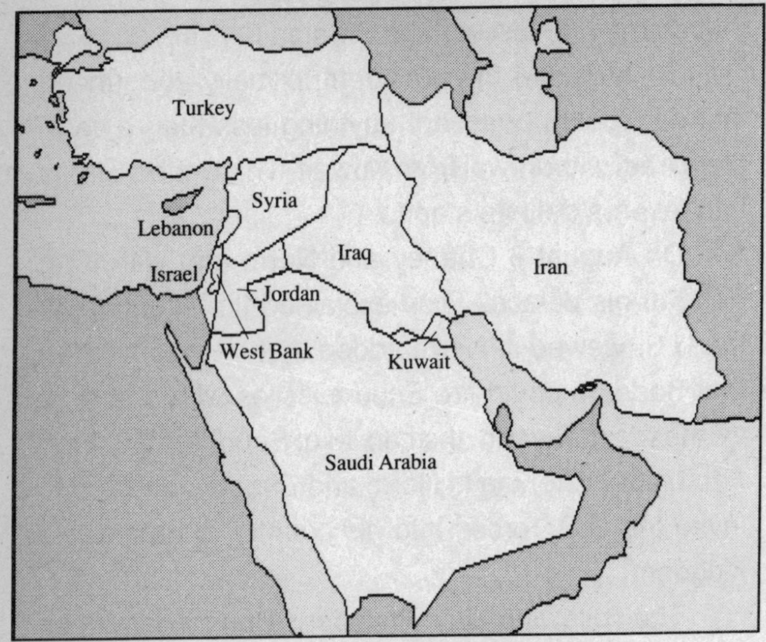

The Middle East.

addition, more than fifty countries committed financial support to help finance Operation Desert Storm.

Shortly after President Bush's announcement about Desert Shield, the U.N. Security Council approved Resolution 661, prohibiting all U.N. members from buying oil from Iraq. A few days later U.N. Security Resolution 662 formally declared that Iraq's invasion of Kuwait was illegal. In response Iraq closed its borders and announced that foreign officials would not be allowed to leave.

When Norm got ready to leave Tampa to go to Saudi Arabia, he called his family together. He told them what was going to happen and explained that it was his job to go, and that he felt proud to do so. He said he wanted them to be proud, too.

By the end of August, there were only 2,300 soldiers from the Eighty-second Airborne Division in Saudi Arabia and the Marines were not even in place yet. Norm talked tough about his soldiers publicly, but he was really bluffing. If Saddam had attacked then, the American soldiers would never have stood a chance. They were so few and they lacked heavy weapons and air support.

By the end of September, Norm began to feel confident about his forces for real. He had more than 100,000 troops as well as over 150,000 tons of weapons, vehicles, equipment, and supplies. The other coalition countries had also started to move in soldiers and weapons. Planes had been landing in Saudi Arabia every seven minutes, as soldiers and weapons arrived from all directions at all hours. Saddam's forces still greatly outnumbered the coalition forces, but within less than two months they had built up a strong defensive presence.

Efforts to get Iraq to leave Kuwait peacefully

continued. The United Nations imposed an embargo, which is a government order that prevents foreign ships from entering or leaving Iraq. Economic sanctions were also imposed. This meant that Iraq could not buy anything from any foreign countries—not even food. Iraq also could not sell anything to U.N. members, such as oil, in order to make money to finance its military machine. It was hoped that these actions would pressure Saddam to remove his forces from Kuwait.

At an historic meeting between President Bush and Soviet President Mikhail Gorbachev, the Soviets declared that they would not disagree with the U.S. policy in the gulf. Although the U.S.S.R. had supported Iraq in the war against Iran, and was responsible for supplying the Iraqis with much of their sophisticated weaponry, they had decided they could no longer back Iraq. The U.S.S.R. was not a member of the allied coalition, but they were not opposed to it. This was a dramatic change from the past, when the two super powers had viewed each other as enemies.

At this time Saddam allowed some groups of Westerners to leave Kuwait and fly home. About one hundred Americans were still being held at important civilian and military sites in Iraq, however. Saddam

Holy War

The Arab word for this is *jihad*, which means "struggle." A holy war is based on the idea that all followers of the prophet Mohammed have a duty to spread the Islamic faith, even through the use of force. They are taught that Islam is the only true faith and that people who practice other religions can be killed if they do not submit to Islam. During the Crusades of the Middle Ages, the Christian armies felt that they could do the same thing to their Arab enemies.

called them "guests." The U.S. Defense Department called them "human shields." By placing the Americans in those specific spots, Saddam was clearly trying to keep the U.S. from bombing certain areas. It was an underhanded move, illegal according to the Geneva Conventions, the series of treaties signed in Geneva, Switzerland, that call for the humane treatment of all soldiers and civilians during wartime. With his human shields in position, Saddam announced to his people that they were to prepare for a "holy war."

Norm was impressed with the troops in America's army. He found them well-trained and motivated. They worked ten-hour days seven days a week in the 120 degree heat of the desert. He was also impressed by the amount of American support the troops were getting. The soldiers received letters, packages, and baked goods from home. It was a big change from their treatment during the Vietnam War.

Norm believed in training and he knew that keeping his soldiers busy would also keep them from being bored and missing home. He also knew from experience that training saves lives.

By mid-October, after ten weeks of buildup, the coalition ground forces were ready. American troops positioned themselves behind a thin line of Saudi troops, who were located a few miles back from Iraqi and Kuwaiti forces. The Marines were positioned east of Saudi Arabia, facing Kuwait, behind another thin line of Saudi forces. Battle lines were drawn slightly to the west, facing the front line with Iraq and Iraq-occupied Kuwait.

In late October, Norm drew up the plan for the operation. The point of the strategy was for coalition forces to trick Saddam into thinking their attack was coming solely from the east. But the bulk of the attack would really be coming from the west. That way Saddam's forces would be dug in with their heavy artillery and tanks facing east while Norm's forces attacked Iraq's undefended border from the west. Before Saddam would even have a chance to make a move, he and his forces would be surrounded.

The essence of Norm's plan was deception. He remembered it had worked well in World War II at El Alamein, the most famous desert battle of all time. Bernard Law Montgomery, an English general, had beaten Erwin Rommel, a German general, who had many more forces. The key was that Montgomery led Rommel to believe that the main attack was coming from one place when it was really coming from someplace else. Surprise is the most important element in desert warfare.

From studying Iraq's war with Iran, Norm and his commanders knew that Iraq believed in a strong defense. This meant that the Iraqis liked to fight from behind fortifications. U.S. intelligence revealed that in the Persian Gulf situation, the first layer of Iraq's defense was made up of divisions along the Kuwaiti coast and Saudi-Kuwaiti border. For up to four miles in front of these lines, Iraqi engineers had laid barbed wire, tank traps, sand barriers, and mine fields.

The 150,000-man Republican Guard, the best fighters of the Iraqi army, were at the rear. They were also the best equipped with artillery, aircraft batteries, and T-72 Soviet tanks. Norm considered them the "center of gravity" of Saddam's forces, and he had his sights set on them. He planned to get them to leave their positions so they would be facing the wrong way when the coalition launched its main attack.

Norm believed that the desert terrain could actually work in his favor when he tried to surround Saddam's forces. He planned to block off every escape route open to them except for one. With only one route open, west along the Euphrates River, Norm predicted that the Iraqi commanders would choose to keep their forces concentrated in order to make a quick getaway if they felt it was necessary. And with the Iraqi tanks all bunched up together, they could be hit more easily by U.S. aircraft. Then if the Iraqi forces spread out to avoid the air attack, they would find themselves face-to-face with coalition ground forces.

By early November the air campaign had been carefully planned. Norm convinced the Air Force in Washington to let his staff in Saudi Arabia decide on all the details of the plan. This would prevent generals who were thousands of miles away from making decisions about things they could not see.

At the end of November, President and Mrs. Bush came to Saudi Arabia and celebrated Thanksgiving with the troops. In describing Norm's state of mind at that time, Bush used one word: "comfortable." He said Norm was comfortable with the Saudis and comfortable with the troops. During his visit Bush declared that the U.S. had been patient with Saddam so far, but the patience wouldn't last forever.

True to Bush's words, U.N. Resolution 678 was passed on November 29. It authorized the use of force against Iraq if they did not withdraw their forces from Kuwait by January 15, 1991. The ultimatum had been delivered.

Norm worked seventeen-hour days in his office, otherwise known as the War Room, four floors below the Saudi Ministry of Defense. There were four different maps on the walls, including one marked with the location of friendly troops and one intelligence map that showed where the enemy forces were located. On a table was the red phone with which he talked to Colin Powell at least once a day; sometimes they spoke up to three to four times a day. On the table Norm also displayed a wind-up grizzly bear that had a yellow ribbon tied around its neck. It was a Christmas gift from his sister Sally. Nicknamed the "Bear" by his troops for his famous temper as well as his size, Norm received quite a few stuffed bears while he was in Saudi Arabia.

Christmas was a hard time for all the troops, as well as for their families back home. Brenda Schwarzkopf began working overtime with the military support groups she had been involved in since the first troops had been sent to the gulf back in August. Her special support group was a walking group. They walked a 4.7 mile course around MacDill Air Force Base every morning. Brenda said that she and the other military wives talked about their worries and fears for their husbands, sons, and daughters in the gulf and about how much they loved and missed them. They traded photos and shared the information available to them about what the troops were doing in Saudi Arabia.

A true general, Norm sent Christmas presents to his family with instructions as to how they should be given out. He sent them gold bracelets, or *cartouches*, which spelled out each person's name in Egyptian hieroglyphics. His family sent him small gifts, but saved the big ones for his return, which they kept under a small tree decorated with lights.

As time ticked slowly by, Norm was busy being a soldier and a diplomat. He met with Arab sultans to discuss the presence of so many Western soldiers in a land with very different customs. Norm knew how important it was that his troops do nothing to offend the Saudis, who were hosting them.

Saudi culture, like all Arab society, is very different from American culture, especially in its treatment of women. Arab women are viewed as sacred according to Islam, the religion of most Arab countries. Islamic women are not supposed to appear in public unless they are wearing long, heavy robes that cover them from head to toe. They are also not allowed to go anywhere alone without a chaperon and they are not allowed to hold jobs.

The female soldiers had a difficult time in Saudi Arabia. They could only use the rear entrances of certain buildings and could not exercise in the same gyms as the male soldiers. They also could not go anywhere unless they were escorted.

Because Islam forbids the drinking of alcohol, Norm forbade all his soldiers from drinking and from reading "adult" magazines. Soldiers dubbed the war the "square war," since they had to be so well-behaved.

An exercise enthusiast, Norm brought his stationary cross-country skiing machine to Saudi Arabia. He kept it in his bedroom, a small room off the War Room. His bed was covered with a camouflage

Norm accompanies Saudi Arabian King Fahd as he reviews U.S. troops, January 6, 1991. (B. Daugherty/AP/Wide World, 1991)

poncho liner that he had slept in every night in Vietnam. Next to his bed was a loaded shotgun, piles of books and magazines, and pictures of his family, plus a copy of the Bible covered in camouflage.

As Norm and his troops prepared for war, the January 15 deadline for Iraqi withdrawal drew closer. On January 9 U.S. Secretary of State James Baker met with Iraqi foreign minister Aziz in Geneva to discuss the situation. He failed to make any progress.

The following day Congress began to debate a declaration of war. On January 12 the U.S. Senate voted 52 to 47 and the House of Representatives voted 250 to 183 to authorize President Bush to use force against Iraq.

On the morning of Tuesday, January 15 President Bush signed a document called a national security directive. It authorized Norm to implement his plan, unless Iraq changed its mind.

But Iraq did not leave Kuwait. Norm did not have to be told that the time had come. Describing his feelings, he paraphrased General Robert E. Lee, who had led the Confederate Army during the Civil War: "The military is the only calling I know that demands that you kill those you love the most: To be a good commander you must love your soldiers; to be a good commander you must send them out to die."

So send them he did. In the early hours of the morning of January 17, the most massive air campaign in the history of the United States began. Operation Desert Shield had become Operation Desert Storm.

5

Operation Desert Storm

It was three hours before dawn on January 17 when the Desert Storm air campaign began. More than one thousand fighter planes took off from ships and bases in the Persian Gulf and Red Sea.

The news that the Persian Gulf War had begun reached the United States at about 8:00 P.M. that evening. Television stations all around the nation began broadcasting that the bombing of Baghdad had started. People were glued to their television sets, shocked that the conflict they had been hearing about for so many months had finally begun. Most did not know that Domino's Pizza in Washington, D.C., had put out a warning at five o'clock that morning. They said that war was likely later that day because they had noticed a record number of pizza deliveries to the White House and Pentagon the night before.

Within minutes after Brenda Schwarzkopf heard the news on TV, her phone rang. It was her husband. She told him that she had just heard missiles were headed for Riyadh, Saudi Arabia.

Norm was safe in his underground bunker four floors below the ground. He remained very calm. "Brenda, it's okay," he said. "Everything is all right. I just wanted to call and let you know that the air war has started, but everything is going to be all right." After that he talked to his children. He closed with three words that would become their family slogan for the rest of the conflict: "Hang in there."

Bombing missions were launched around the clock. In the first forty-eight hours of the war, the air forces of the United States, Great Britain, France, Italy, Saudi Arabia, and Kuwait, flew 2,107 combat missions. Each day they dropped as many as five thousand tons of bombs on Baghdad, Iraq. Pilots said the flashing lights of the antiaircraft fire over Baghdad reminded them of a Fourth of July fireworks display.

The coalition also pounded targets throughout Kuwait and Iraq, based on a 600-page daily computerized assignment book. Within those first few days,

Baghdad's electricity and water supplies were knocked out, as well as their military and civilian communications systems. This made it even more difficult for Saddam Hussein to figure out what his enemies were doing. Although the coalition had assumed that he was expecting an air attack, Saddam appeared not to be ready for it. Some said it might have been because he thought the coalition had been only bluffing about attacking Iraq. Others said he might not have had any idea what a modern air war was like.

In those first forty-eight hours, the attacking forces lost only seven planes, a very low number, considering the number of missions flown. Casualties were also low. Norm said afterwards that one of his greatest moments was day one of the air campaign, when the planes came home and there was so little loss of human life.

Of the 4,000 bombing sorties that had been flown, eighty percent were said to have been effective. A sortie is one flight by one airplane. Because of modern technology, pilots were able to hit their targets within twenty feet or closer. This was quite different from bombing missions of past wars. During World War II bombers were considered successful if they got within a half a mile of their targets. Even during the Vietnam War in the 1960s, pilots of the high altitude B-52 bombers were happy to get within a quarter mile of their targets. The computerized weaponry used by coalition forces seemed like something out of a science fiction movie to many Americans who watched the TV news reports.

Norm gave his first press conference at 7:00 A.M., Saudi time, on January 18. He informed the American public about the eighty percent success rate of the initial bombing campaign, and the professionalism of all the fighting forces. Then he turned the podium over to Lieutenant General Horner, who showed videos of some of the bombing sorties. One showed the precision bombing of a Scud missile storehouse in Kuwait. An allied pilot had sent two thousand-pound bombs right through the storehouse door.

Some reporters worried that the news videos of the bombings made war look like a Nintendo video game. They felt it was important to make sure the public saw the uglier side of war and understood that people were actually being killed.

Norm was angered by the reporters' criticism. He knew only too well just how deadly war can be. He pointed out that the newscasts were not at all frivolous and that no one involved in the war took it anything but seriously.

Norm admitted that he had been scared when the war began. But he didn't feel scared by the Scud missiles the Iraqis were firing. For one thing they were not very effective missiles. Besides that, the Scuds had to be launched from platforms. According to U.S. intelligence reports, all the Iraqi launching sites had been destroyed by the end of the second day of the war. Norm said he would be more scared of being outside during a thunderstorm in Georgia than of standing in the streets of Riyadh when the Scuds were coming down. This was reassuring to King Fahd, who was worried about what the missiles would do to his country.

Saddam did have some surprises up his sleeve, however. He had a number of movable Scud launchers that the coalition did not know about. Just over twenty-four hours into the war, Saddam launched eight Scud missiles at Tel Aviv and Haifa, two cities in Israel. Most exploded without causing any harm, but one injured two people.

Norm and the allies now had a major problem. They had to prevent Israel from retaliating against Iraq. By bombing Israel Saddam was clearly trying to

Arab-Israeli Conflict

Palestine, described as the land of Canaan in the Bible, has seen much warfare in the last two thousand years. Arabs and Jews have lived there for centuries, and both say that the land belongs to them. In 1949 the Jews of Palestine set up an independent state called Israel. Immediately, the neighboring Arab states of Jordan, Egypt, Iraq, Lebanon, and Syria attacked the new nation, saying that it had no right to exist. In the fighting, many Palestinian Arabs were driven from their homes. Since then Israel has fought and won four wars with its Arab neighbors. In 1973 the United Nations decided that Palestinians had the right to govern themselves, but Israel would not agree to give up territory so that the Palestinians could have their own country. With little hope of defeating Israel or setting up a Palestinian state, Arabs launched terrorist attacks on Israel. But with American support, the four million people of Israel survived this terrorism. Finally, in 1979, Egypt signed a peace treaty with Israel. However, other Arab nations refused to do the same. Four years later, the Palestinians agreed that Israel had a right to exist and said that they were giving up terrorism. Yet that has not solved the problem. Arab nations still do not want Israel to exist. Nor does Israel want a Palestinian state.

turn the war into an Arab-Israeli conflict.

The Arabs and the Israelis had been fighting on and off since the founding of Israel in 1949. There had always been tension between Israel and its surrounding Arab neighbors. Saddam knew that if he could get Israel to attack Iraq, this could weaken the coalition. Syria, Egypt, and Saudi Arabia might decide to stop fighting if their traditional enemy, Israel, was suddenly on their side.

Two hours after the Scud attacks on Israel, there were two loud bangs. In the sky over Riyadh, two streaks of light shot upward. They were the first American Patriot missiles on their way to intercept another Scud. Patriots had been designed to hit enemy missiles in the air before they hit their targets, but they had never been tested in an actual war before. The first time they were fired, they worked perfectly.

On January 19 three more Iraqi Scuds hit Israel. Seventeen people were injured. So far Iraq had not used poison gas, but many people thought Saddam would. It was clear that he was intent on drawing Israel into the conflict. To prevent this and to help protect the country, the United States immediately supplied Israel with Patriot missile systems, as well as American crews to operate them.

That same day in Baghdad, Saddam paraded captured allied pilots on television, stating that they would be used as human shields. The pilots looked terrible. Their faces were puffed up and had red marks as if they had been beaten. The American public was shocked and angry. Norm termed Saddam a "thug." Saddam's actions were another clear violation of the Geneva Conventions' laws about the humane treatment of prisoners. But Saddam did not care. This was his holy war and he would do anything.

By the end of the first week of war, the coalition forces had knocked out almost all of the Iraqi air bases. Not a single one of Saddam's planes had shot down an allied plane. A total of nineteen allied planes had been lost to antiaircraft fire. Only six Americans had been killed in action, one wounded, and fourteen captured. Norm's forces controlled the skies. Back in the U.S., President Bush announced that Operation Desert Storm was proceeding right on schedule.

Despite the destruction to his forces, Saddam was not about to give up. At the beginning of that first week of war, he opened valves at Kuwaiti oil refineries and began spilling oil into the gulf. President Bush called Saddam an environmental terrorist. The oil spill threatened to contaminate the entire area's water supply and killed fish and other wildlife. This seriously damaged the food supply for the six million people who live in the Persian Gulf region.

In late January Saddam's forces finally engaged the coalition's ground forces for the first time. An Iraqi force of seven hundred men occupied the abandoned Saudi oil refining town of Khafji, eight miles south of the Kuwaiti border. This made the Saudis angry. King Fahd asked for help to recover the town.

The Americans quickly stepped in. After a two-day ground battle, two hundred Iraqis were killed and four hundred taken prisoner. By January 31 the Saudis controlled Khafji again. Eleven American Marines died during the fighting. Seven of the deaths were caused by friendly fire, when an armored vehicle containing seven Marines was hit by a missile fired from an allied plane.

Norm quickly defended the pilot who had fired the missile. He also grieved for the soldiers who had been killed. Watching tapes of the PBS *Civil War* series that Colin Powell had sent him helped him to realize that other generals had known how he was feeling. It reassured him that these generals too had cried over the loss of human life.

Norm's long hours in the War Room prevented him from seeing his troops as much as he would have liked. When he could, he went to visit his soldiers at their posts throughout Saudi Arabia. Four Black Hawk helicopters always accompanied him on these trips. Norm was the one who chose which helicopter to ride in just before each flight. That way no one could know which one he would be riding in and sabotage the aircraft. A squad of security men surrounded him. All the guards spoke fluent Arabic and carried M-16 rifles equipped with silencers. Behind him an executive officer carried his briefcase. Another aide carried Norm's rucksack, which was filled with a protective chemical warfare suit. A sergeant carried a sixty-pound backpack that held Norm's satellite relay hookup. This enabled him to make contact with any spot on the globe within seconds.

Norm visited air bases in eastern and central Saudi Arabia that had been hit repeatedly by Scud missiles. He told the soldiers there that they were America's heroes. Then he invited them to ask questions. Wherever he went, he posed for pictures with the troops. He had lunch at the mobile lunch stands that offered free burgers, hot dogs, french fries, and sodas. He sat at tables with the troops and autographed helmets. He also made a point of always asking the soldiers if they knew why they were in Saudi Arabia.

Norm with the troops at a Patriot missile base, January 29, 1991. (D. Turnley/Detroit Free Press/Black Star, 1991)

Norm missed his family greatly. He was thrilled to see Brenda on television when President Bush gave his State of the Union address on January 29, 1991. As she was introduced, there was a lot of applause. Norm said he was proud of Brenda and all of the military families she was representing.

The air war continued. Norm knew that the troops were beginning to get impatient to either fight a ground war or go home. No matter how successful the air campaign might be, Norm believed the ground campaign would eventually be needed. He feared it, as everyone else feared it, because he was aware that many lives could be lost. He could only hope that the plans he and his staff had worked out would save lives. Norm had originally predicted that the ground war would start at the end of February. As it turned out, he was right on target.

Defense Secretary Cheney and General Powell flew into Riyadh on February 9. Norm met with them for over eight hours. Two days later Cheney advised President Bush that Norm wanted to set February 21 as the date for the ground invasion. A day later, Norm changed the date to February 24, 4:00 A.M., Saudi time.

On February 23 President Bush gave Saddam

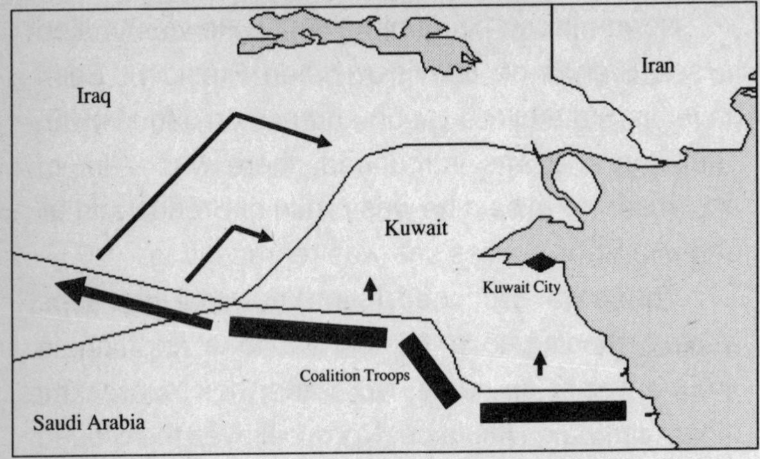

***Tactical Map**: Norm's deception plan positioned coalition troops along the Kuwaiti border. When the aerial bombings began, a number of the troops shifted west along the Iraqi border. When the ground assault started, these troops came up through Iraq and around the side of the Iraqi troops in Kuwait. The rest of the troops moved north into Kuwait.*

twenty-four hours to begin a complete withdrawal from Kuwait. Instead of withdrawing, Saddam set fire to hundreds of Kuwaiti oil wells. This was his second act of environmental terrorism. Millions of barrels of oil went up in smoke and the entire gulf area became severely polluted. The extent of the damage still is not known. Iraqi soldiers also started executing Kuwaitis in the streets. On top of that, ten minutes before the deadline set by President Bush was to expire, Saddam sent another Scud missile into Israel.

The night of February 23 was cold and overcast in Saudi Arabia. According to plan, at 4:00 A.M., Norm signaled the beginning of the ground war. At that very moment, Radio Baghdad in Iraq played the popular Elton John song, "Saturday Night's All Right [For Fighting]."

Within two and a half hours, Marine divisions had broken through the first line of the Iraqi defense. Twenty hours later they were almost in Kuwait. At the same time, more than 5,500 Iraqis had been taken prisoner. The thirty-eight-day air war had badly damaged Saddam's forces. His tanks had been cut to less than half their original number, almost fifty percent of his artillery was gone, and many of his aircraft had been destroyed.

Norm's deception plan met with even more success. First the 101st Airborne Division flew fifty miles into Iraq and took control of a sixty-square mile area. Two thousand more soldiers arrived that night. American and British troops from three divisions attacked closer to Kuwait, and cut off Iraqi supply lines. Other French and American troops advanced thirty miles into Iraq, moving in the direction of the Euphrates river. Saddam's forces were being surrounded. Soon they would have no way out.

Norm during a press briefing in Riyadh, February 27, 1991. (G. Gibson/AP/Wide World, 1991)

Within two days many allied soldiers had crossed the border into Iraq and Kuwait. Kuwaiti and Arab forces arrived first, with the Americans following behind. More kept coming. Kuwaiti men, women, and children cheered and yelled, "Thank you" to the allied troops. The number of enemy prisoners had risen to twenty thousand, and it kept rising. Many Iraqi soldiers surrendered voluntarily, actually glad to see the allies. Some said in broken English, "George Bush good." Then they mentioned the name Saddam Hussein, and proceeded to make slitting motions across their throats. Many of them had been living in terrible conditions with no food or water. One was reported to have been surviving on rain water and grass for a week. The allies gave all the surrendering Iraqi soldiers food, water, cigarettes, a shower, and a change of clothes.

That night Saddam got back at the coalition. An Iraqi Scud hit an allied barracks that housed about one hundred troops, mostly reserves who had arrived in Saudi Arabia only recently. Twenty-eight soldiers were killed, including three women, the first women to die in the war.

The following day allied troops took over the U.S. Embassy in Kuwait City. There was a fierce battle at Kuwait International Airport.

In Iraq American troops reached the Euphrates River and advanced to meet the Republican Guard head on. The Republican Guard was totally unprepared for the attack. Some of their tanks were actually facing the wrong way, just as Norm had hoped when he had originally conceived his deception plan. In thick mud in the falling darkness, eight hundred American tanks fought almost three hundred Republican Guard tanks, while American aircraft pounded the Iraqis from the sky. It was the largest tank battle since World War II, and it lasted through the night. When the sun rose the next morning, Saddam's Republican Guard was finished.

By day four the American Marines had taken over Kuwait International Airport. There were an estimated forty to fifty thousand prisoners. Black smoke filled the air over Kuwait City as the torched oil wells continued to burn. The number of Iraqi dead was somewhere between sixty to one hundred thousand. Fifty-six Americans had also lost their lives in the ground war. But the coalition forces were overwhelmingly victorious. Although the fighting continued, Operation Desert Storm had achieved its primary objective.

Norm emerged from his underground bunker to appear before television cameras. He wore his customary battle fatigues and explained the ground war in detail to reporters and the public. He used his pointer and flip charts to illustrate what he had to say.

He invited questions when he was finished. When one reporter asked Norm what he thought of Saddam as a military strategist, Norm ticked off points on the fingers of his left hand as he said that Saddam was "neither a strategist, nor is he schooled in the operational art, nor is he a tactician, nor is he a general, nor is he a soldier." After running out of fingers, he added, "Other than that, he's a great military man."

Norm attributed the success of the war to the fighting spirit of the coalition forces and the new high-tech equipment of the American Army. He praised the integration of ground and air power, known as "AirLand Battle." This time the joint operations of the Army, Navy, Air Force, and Marines had gone off smoothly. It was a far cry from the problems the U.S. had experienced during Operation Urgent Fury in Grenada.

The U.S. had one important revolutionary weapon—stealth aircraft—that Norm and many other people felt was the key to the landslide victory. These fighter-bombers could slip undetected past Iraqi radar and drop their bombs. They could look far behind enemy lines without being detected and report back on enemy operations. In addition, the U.S. had computers that could track incoming tank and artillery rounds so fast they could wipe out the enemy before they were even able to fire a second shot.

Norm's briefing was viewed by millions of people in the United States. President Bush did not get to see most of it, however. He was busy preparing to give the speech that would formally end the war. Bush had met with Chairman Powell that afternoon and they both agreed the time had come. Chairman Powell then called Norm, who also agreed.

At nine o'clock that night President Bush addressed the nation. "Kuwait is liberated. Iraq's army is defeated . . . Exactly one hundred hours since ground operations commenced, and six weeks since the start of Operation Desert Storm, all United States and coalition forces will suspend offensive combat operations." Operation Desert Storm had come to an end. But not for Norm. As chief commanding officer, he still had things to do.

On the morning of March 3, Norm flew by helicopter to a captured Iraqi airfield, three miles north of the Kuwaiti border. The wind was filled with black smoke from burning oil wells. His mission was to meet with a delegation of Iraqi generals to discuss the ceasefire. He knew it was important to make sure that the Iraqis were not humiliated at the meeting.

The eight Iraqi generals were all wearing their dress uniforms. Norm was wearing what he had worn throughout the conflict—his camouflage fatigues. He gave the order that everyone present was to be electronically searched. One Iraqi general said that he did not like the idea.

Norm turned to the general and said, "Well, that's the way it's going to be and I'll go first."

The Iraqis wanted to know who had given the order. They were informed that General Schwarzkopf had. Then they wanted to know where he was and why the man in camouflage fatigues and boots who had just been searched was telling them what to do. When it was finally made clear to them that the man in khaki was General Schwarzkopf, they were shocked.

After some discussion, the Iraqis agreed to accept all of the United Nations resolutions and they agreed to return all of their prisoners of war. Norm informed reporters that he felt a lasting peace was on the way.

The next day Norm bid farewell to the first of his front-line troops who were heading for home. He told them to tell their war stories, but not to forget to credit all of the forces who had helped, including the Air Force and the Navy, along with British, French, Italian, and Arab troops.

Later, when asked what it felt like to be a national hero, Norm shook his head and said he was not a hero. Then he added, "It doesn't take a hero to order men into battle. It takes a hero to go into battle. These are the people who deserve adulation." He also said that the allies had one important advantage over the Iraqis—the support of the rest of the world. That had made all the difference, along with the "fighting spirit of individuals going into combat," with which he said wars had been won since ancient times.

On April 23, after almost nine months in the gulf, Norm finally came home. He retired from active duty in June 1991, having served thirty-five years in the Army. With the triumph of the Persian Gulf victory behind him, General H. Norman Schwarzkopf will go down in history as one of the greatest American generals who ever lived.

Quick Facts

Weapons of the Gulf War

The Patriot Missile: This seventeen-and-a-half foot missile, designed to shoot down high-speed aircraft and missiles, can fly three times the speed of sound and reach an altitude of fifteen miles. Most of the Scud missiles fired by Iraq were shot down by Patriot missiles. They were known by the coalition soldiers as "Scud Busters."

The Scud Ballistic Missile: This twenty-foot missile was first produced in the 1960s by the Russians. It can carry its explosive warhead as far as 575 miles.The Scud loses accuracy as it travels farther, so it is not very effective against troops on the ground. Iraq used it as a weapon of terror.

"Smart" Bombs: When one of these bombs is dropped from an aircraft, someone in the plane guides the bomb's flight by watching a television picture or aiming a laser beam at the target. A "smart" bomb is very accurate.

The Stealth Fighter: This single-seat, twin-engined aircraft is shaped like a large, flat arrowhead. It is designed to be almost invisible to radar and the naked eye. The Stealth attacked heavily defended Iraqi targets with smart bombs and missiles, but not one plane was shot down.

Chronology

1934 On August 22 Norm is born in Trenton, New Jersey.

1946 Norm goes to Iran to join his father.

1952 Norm starts at the United States Military Academy at West Point.

1956 Norm graduates from West Point.

1957 In March Norm is assigned to the 101st Airborne Division.

1960 In July Norm serves as aide-de-camp for the commanding general of the Berlin command.

1964 Norm receives his Masters degree from USC.

1965 In June Norm is sent to Vietnam as an adviser.

1968 In July Norm marries Brenda Hoslinger.
In August Norm is promoted to lieutenant colonel.

1969 In December Norm is sent back to Vietnam for his second tour of duty.

1972 In August Norm goes to the Army War College at Carlisle Barracks, Pennsylvania.

1974 In October Norm becomes the deputy commander at Fort Richardson, Alaska.

1976 In October Norm is appointed commander at Fort Lewis, Washington.

1978 In July Norm is appointed to serve at Camp H. M. Smith in Hawaii.

1980 In August Norm is sent to Mainz, West Germany to be assistant division commander.

1983 In June Norm is assigned to command the Twenty-fourth Infantry at Fort Stewart.
On October 23 Norm is chosen as deputy commander for Operation Urgent Fury.

1986 In June Norm is promoted to lieutenant general and is commander at Fort Lewis.

1988 In November Norm is awarded his fourth star and becomes commander in chief of CentCom.

1990 On August 2 Saddam attacks Kuwait.
On August 5 President Bush declares that Iraq must withdraw from Kuwait.
On August 7 President Bush sends American troops to the gulf.
On November 29 U.N. Resolution 678 is passed, authorizing the use of force against Iraq if they do not withdraw by January 15.

1991 On January 12 the U.S. Congress authorizes President Bush to use force against Iraq.
On January 17 the air campaign begins.
On February 24 the ground war begins.
On February 27 President Bush announces that all the U.S. and coalition forces will suspend offensive combat operations.
On March 3 Norm meets with a delegation of Iraqi generals and they agree to all of the U.N. requests.
On April 23 Norm returns home.

Index

Ace Card Chulitna, 41
airborne, 21, 25, 28, 49, 66, 90
artillery, 18, 20, 28, 35, 69-70, 90, 94

Bush, George, 62-65, 67, 72, 76, 84, 88-89, 91, 94-95

Cheney, Richard, 62-64, 88
coalition, 64, 66-67, 69, 71, 78-81, 83-85, 92-95

Duc Co, 28

Fort Benning, GA, 21, 24
Fort Campbell, KY, 21-23
Fort Lewis, WA, 43, 46, 54
Fort Richardson, AK, 41
Fort Stewart, GA, 45-47, 53-55
France, 3, 6, 64-65, 78, 90, 96

"Gangbusters", 9, 15-16
Great Britain, 3, 6, 48, 50, 78, 90, 96
Grenada, 47-48, 50, 52-53, 94

Holy War, 70
human shield, 68, 84
Hussein, Saddam, 60-61, 63-64, 66-69, 71-72, 79, 81-85, 89-93

Ia Drang Valley, 28
infantry, 18, 20-24, 32, 36, 41, 43-45, 53, 55
Iran, 9-11, 58-60, 63, 67, 70

Iraq, 5, 58-65, 67-72, 75-76, 78-79, 81-85, 89-97
  Baghdad, 6, 77-79, 83, 90
Islam, 70, 74
Israel, 81-83, 90
Italy, 6, 78, 96

Joint Chiefs of Staff, 58, 61

King Fahd, 63-64, 81, 85
Kuwait, 6, 58-62, 64-65, 67, 69-70, 72, 76, 78, 80, 84-85, 89-93, 95

Lee, Robert E., 2, 17, 76
Lindbergh kidnapping, 9-10

MacDill Airforce Base, FL, 57, 73
Mainz, W. Germany, 44-45
mechanical engineering, 17, 24
Metcalf, Joseph, III, 47, 50-52
Mullen, Michael, 35, 37

National Security Council, 58, 62

oil, 59-63, 65, 67, 84-85, 89, 93, 95
Operation Desert Shield, 57, 61, 64-65, 76
Operation Desert Storm, 5-7, 65, 76-77, 84, 93, 95
Operation Urgent Fury, 39, 46-47, 94

Pentagon, 35-36, 39, 44-45, 47, 54-55, 59, 61, 78
Persian Gulf, 57, 61, 64, 77

Persian Gulf War, 4-5, 64, 70, 77, 97
Powell, Colin, 61-62, 72, 85, 88, 95
purple heart, 26, 29

Republican Guard, 70, 92-93

Saudi Arabia, 6, 58, 60, 62-63, 65-66, 69, 71-75, 78, 83, 86-88, 90, 92
  Riyadh, 5, 64, 78, 81, 83, 88
Schwarzkopf, Brenda, 31-32, 37, 43, 73, 78, 88
Schwarzkopf, Christian, 44, 55, 59, 70
Schwarzkopf, Herbert Norman, 7-11, 13
Schwarzkopf, Sally, 7, 37, 72
Scud, 64, 80-81, 83, 86, 90, 92
silver star, 26, 29, 32-34

U. N. Security Council, 62, 65
U.S. Central Command (CentCom), 56-59, 62
U.S.S.R., 3, 48, 67

Valley Forge Military Academy, 14
Vietnam, 21, 24-29, 31-32, 34-38, 53, 68, 75, 80

War Room, 5, 72, 75, 85
Washington, D.C., 31, 39, 77
West Point Military Academy, 3-4, 7-9, 14-19, 21, 24, 31
World War I, 8
World War II, 3, 9, 69, 79, 93

About the Author

E.J. Valentine is the creator of a number of children's books. She has also written television and music videos for kids. One of her grandfathers was a World War I soldier who was awarded a purple heart, and the other was a World War II colonel. A runner and a weightlifter, she hopes someday to meet Norm and go skeet shooting with him.